Books by Randall Jarrell

POETRY

The Rage for the Lost Penny (in *Five Young American Poets*)	1940
Blood for a Stranger	1942
Little Friend, Little Friend	1945
Losses	1948
The Seven-League Crutches	1951
Selected Poems	1955
The Woman at the Washington Zoo	1960
The Lost World	1965
The Complete Poems	1969
Selected Poems	1990

ESSAYS

Poetry and the Age	1953
A Sad Heart at the Supermarket	1962
The Third Book of Criticism	1969
Kipling, Auden & Co.	1980

FICTION

Pictures from an Institution	1954

CHILDREN'S BOOKS

The Gingerbread Rabbit	1964
The Bat-Poet	1964
The Animal Family	1965
Fly by Night	1976

TRANSLATIONS

The Golden Bird and Other Fairy Tales of the Brothers Grimm	1962
The Rabbit Catcher and Other Fairy Tales of Ludwig Bechstein	1962
The Three Sisters	1969
Faust, Part I	1976

ANTHOLOGIES

The Anchor Book of Stories	1958
The Best Short Stories of Rudyard Kipling	1961
The English in England (Kipling stories)	1963
In the Vernacular: The English in India (Kipling stories)	1963
Six Russian Short Novels	1963

RANDALL JARRELL
SELECTED POEMS

RANDALL JARRELL

SELECTED POEMS

Edited by William H. Pritchard

MICHAEL DI CAPUA BOOKS

FARRAR, STRAUS AND GIROUX

NEW YORK

CONTENTS

FOREWORD

This selection of fifty poems by Randall Jarrell (his three-part poem, "The Lost World," is counted as one poem) attempts to put the best possible case for his value and importance as a member of the post–World War II generation of American poets. To my own eyes and ears, he ranks with Robert Lowell and Elizabeth Bishop as one of the leading poets of that generation; but ranking is less called for than is a recognition of how good Jarrell at his best could be. Such a recognition will not occur so long as he is remembered solely as the author of one heavily anthologized short poem, "The Death of the Ball Turret Gunner," or as a superbly resourceful and endlessly quotable critic of other poets. It is also possible that Jarrell's productivity has told against his reputation as one of the essential poets. His *Complete Poems*, published in 1969, four years after his death, includes not only *Selected Poems* (1955), *The Woman at the Washington Zoo* (1960), and *The Lost World* (1965), but also his uncollected poems and many unpublished poems, as well as those he did not reprint from earlier books.

Jarrell once wrote to Bishop that one should look for the good poems in any poet's work. Even his beloved Rilke, he admitted, was "monstrously self-indulgent a lot of the time." But the good poems made up for it, and, anyway, "one expects most of a good poet's work to be quite bad." The exaggeration, if it is that, surely applies to Jarrell's own work, especially to the poems he wrote at the beginning of his career (1935–1942). That he himself was aware of their insufficiencies is evident from the severity with which he treated his first book, *Blood for a Stranger* (1942), by allowing only ten of its forty-six poems into his *Selected Poems*.

In that 1955 volume, which now forms the first two hundred or so pages of *The Complete Poems*, Jarrell chose—as did Wordsworth before him—to group his poems under certain subject headings.

There is some value in noting which poems he thought belonged to-gether, but there is also a certain quirkiness to the arrangement. This new selection is chronological, by date of publication, and reaches from "90 North" (1941), the poem in which Jarrell first found his distinctive voice, to "The Player Piano," written in 1964, a year before his death, and—in Mary Jarrell's words—"the last fully realized poem he would write."

His friend Lowell spoke nothing less than the truth when he wrote that Jarrell's gifts, "both by nature and by a lifetime of hard dedication and growth, were wit, pathos, and brilliance of intelli-gence." My hope is that readers of this selection, in thinking about Jarrell's gifts as a poet, will find appropriate a sentence from his second essay on Robert Frost:

> To have the distance from the most awful and most nearly
> unbearable parts of the poems, to the most tender, subtle,
> and loving parts, a distance so great; to have this whole range
> of being treated with so much humor and sadness and com-
> posure, with such plain truth; to see that a man can still
> include, connect, and make humanly understandable or hu-
> manly unununderstandable so *much*—this is one of the freshest
> and oldest of joys.

W. H. P.

RANDALL JARRELL
SELECTED POEMS

90 North

At home, in my flannel gown, like a bear to its floe,
I clambered to bed; up the globe's impossible sides
I sailed all night—till at last, with my black beard,
My furs and my dogs, I stood at the northern pole.

There in the childish night my companions lay frozen,
The stiff furs knocked at my starveling throat,
And I gave my great sigh: the flakes came huddling,
Were they really my end? In the darkness I turned to my rest.

—Here, the flag snaps in the glare and silence
Of the unbroken ice. I stand here,
The dogs bark, my beard is black, and I stare
At the North Pole . . .
                          And now what? Why, go back.

Turn as I please, my step is to the south.
The world—my world spins on this final point
Of cold and wretchedness: all lines, all winds
End in this whirlpool I at last discover.

And it is meaningless. In the child's bed
After the night's voyage, in that warm world
Where people work and suffer for the end
That crowns the pain—in that Cloud-Cuckoo-Land

I reached my North and it had meaning.
Here at the actual pole of my existence,
Where all that I have done is meaningless,
Where I die or live by accident alone—

Where, living or dying, I am still alone;
Here where North, the night, the berg of death
Crowd me out of the ignorant darkness,
I see at last that all the knowledge

I wrung from the darkness—that the darkness flung me—
Is worthless as ignorance: nothing comes from nothing,
The darkness from the darkness. Pain comes from the darkness
And we call it wisdom. It is pain.

[1941]

Absent with Official Leave

The lights are beginning to go out in the barracks.
They persist or return, as the wakeful hollow,
But only for a moment; then the windows blacken
For all the hours of the soldier's life.

It is life into which he composes his body.
He covers his ears with his pillow, and begins to drift
(Like the plumes the barracks trail into the sky)
Past the laughs, the quarrels, and the breath of others

To the ignorant countries where civilians die
Inefficiently, in their spare time, for nothing . . .
The curved roads hopping through the aimless green
Dismay him, and the cottages where people cry

For themselves and, sometimes, for the absent soldier—
Who inches through hedges where the hunters sprawl
For birds, for birds; who turns in ecstasy
Before the slow small fires the women light

His charmed limbs, all endearing from the tub.
He dozes, and the washed locks trail like flax
Down the dark face; the unaccusing eyes
That even the dream's eyes are averted from

See the wind puff down the chimney, warm the hands
White with the blossoms it pretends are snow . . .
He moans like a bear in his enchanted sleep,
And the grave mysterious beings of his years—

The causes who mourn above his agony like trees—
Are moved for their child, and bend across his limbs
The one face opening for his life, the eyes
That look without shame even into his.

And the man awakes, and sees around his life
The night that is never silent, broken with the sighs
And patient breathing of the dark companions
With whom he labors, sleeps, and dies.

[1943]

The Carnegie Library, Juvenile Division

The soot drifted from the engines to the marble
The readers climbed to: stone, and the sooty casts
(Dark absent properties confused with crates
And rest-rooms in the darkness of a basement,
And constant in their senseless line, like dates:
A past that puzzles no one, or a child)
All overlooking—as the child too overlooked—
The hills and stone and steeples of the town
Grey in the pure red of the dying sun.

Here under the waves' roof, where the seals are men;
In the rhymes' twilight, where the old cup ticks
Its gnawing lesson; where the beasts loom in the green
Firred darkness of the märchen: country the child thought life
And wished for and crept to out of his own life—
Must you still isle such, raiders from a world
That you so long ago lost heart to represent?
The child tugs the strap tight round four books
To leave the cavern. And the cut-out ornaments
In colors harsh and general as names,
The dolls' scarred furniture, too small
For anything but pity, like the child—
Surely you recognize in these the hole
That widens from the middle of a field
To that one country where the poor see gold?
The woodman dances home, rich, rich; but a shade glides
Into the bright strange sunlight of the world
He owned once; the thaler blur out like a tear,

He knocks like a stranger and a stranger speaks,
And he sees, brass on the knocker, the gnome's joyless smile.

The books too read to ashes—for one owns
Nothing, and finds that there is no exchange
For all the uses lined here, free as air,
Fleeting as air: the sad repeated spell
Of that deep string, half music and half pain—
How many have believed you worth a soul!
How many here will purchase with a world
These worlds still smoldering for the perpetual
Children who haunt this fire-sale of the centuries.
Wandering among so many lives, they too will bear
The life from which they cannot yet escape;
And learn to doubt, with our sad useless smile,
That single universe the living share—
The practice with which even the books are charred.

We learned from you so much about so many things
But never what we were; and yet you made us that.
We found in you the knowledge for a life
But not the will to use it in our lives
That were always, somehow, so different from the books'.
We learn from you to understand, but not to change.

[1944]

A Front

Fog over the base: the beams ranging
From the five towers pull home from the night
The crews cold in fur, the bombers banging
Like lost trucks down the levels of the ice.
A glow drifts in like mist (how many tons of it?),
Bounces to a roll, turns suddenly to steel
And tires and turrets, huge in the trembling light.
The next is high, and pulls up with a wail,
Comes round again—no use. And no use for the rest
In drifting circles out along the range;
Holding no longer, changed to a kinder course,
The flights drone southward through the steady rain.
The base is closed. . . . But one voice keeps on calling,
The lowering pattern of the engines grows;
The roar gropes downward in its shaky orbit
For the lives the season quenches. Here below
They beg, order, are not heard; and hear the darker
Voice rising: *Can't you hear me? Over. Over—*
All the air quivers, and the east sky glows.

[1944]

[9

Losses

It was not dying: everybody died.
It was not dying: we had died before
In the routine crashes—and our fields
Called up the papers, wrote home to our folks,
And the rates rose, all because of us.
We died on the wrong page of the almanac,
Scattered on mountains fifty miles away;
Diving on haystacks, fighting with a friend,
We blazed up on the lines we never saw.
We died like aunts or pets or foreigners.
(When we left high school nothing else had died
For us to figure we had died like.)

In our new planes, with our new crews, we bombed
The ranges by the desert or the shore,
Fired at towed targets, waited for our scores—
And turned into replacements and woke up
One morning, over England, operational.
It wasn't different: but if we died
It was not an accident but a mistake
(But an easy one for anyone to make).
We read our mail and counted up our missions—
In bombers named for girls, we burned
The cities we had learned about in school—
Till our lives wore out; our bodies lay among
The people we had killed and never seen.
When we lasted long enough they gave us medals;
When we died they said, "Our casualties were low."

They said, "Here are the maps"; we burned the cities.

It was not dying—no, not ever dying;
But the night I died I dreamed that I was dead,
And the cities said to me: "Why are you dying?
We are satisfied, if you are; but why did I die?"

[1944]

The Death of the Ball Turret Gunner

From my mother's sleep I fell into the State,
And I hunched in its belly till my wet fur froze.
Six miles from earth, loosed from its dream of life,
I woke to black flak and the nightmare fighters.
When I died they washed me out of the turret with a hose.

[1945]

A Pilot from the Carrier

Strapped at the center of the blazing wheel,
His flesh ice-white against the shattered mask,
He tears at the easy clasp, his sobbing breaths
Misting the fresh blood lightening to flame,
Darkening to smoke; trapped there in pain
And fire and breathlessness, he struggles free
Into the sunlight of the upper sky—
And falls, a quiet bundle in the sky,
The miles to warmth, to air, to waking:
To the great flowering of his life, the hemisphere
That holds his dangling years. In its long slow sway
The world steadies and is almost still. . . .
He is alone; and hangs in knowledge
Slight, separate, estranged: a lonely eye
Reading a child's first scrawl, the carrier's wake—
The travelling milk-like circle of a miss
Beside the plant-like genius of the smoke
That shades, on the little deck, the little blaze
Toy-like as the glitter of the wing-guns,
Shining as the fragile sun-marked plane
That grows to him, rubbed silver tipped with flame.

[1945]

The Dead Wingman

Seen on the sea, no sign; no sign, no sign
In the black firs and terraces of hills
Ragged in mist. The cone narrows, snow
Glares from the bleak walls of a crater. No.
Again the houses jerk like paper, turn,
And the surf streams by: a port of toys
Is starred with its fires and faces; but no sign.

In the level light, over the fiery shores,
The plane circles stubbornly: the eyes distending
With hatred and misery and longing, stare
Over the blackening ocean for a corpse.
The fires are guttering; the dials fall,
A long dry shudder climbs along his spine,
His fingers tremble; but his hard unchanging stare
Moves unacceptingly: *I have a friend.*

The fires are grey; no star, no sign
Winks from the breathing darkness of the carrier
Where the pilot circles for his wingman; where,
Gliding above the cities' shells, a stubborn eye
Among the embers of the nations, achingly
Tracing the circles of that worn, unchanging *No*—
The lives' long war, lost war—the pilot sleeps.

[1945]

The Märchen

(GRIMM'S TALES)

Listening, listening; it is never still.
This is the forest: long ago the lives
Edged armed into its tides (the axes were its stone
Lashed with the skins of dwellers to its boughs);
We felled our islands there, at last, with iron.
The sunlight fell to them, according to our wish,
And we believed, till nightfall, in that wish;
And we believed, till nightfall, in our lives.

The bird is silent; but its cold breast stirs
Raggedly, and the gloom the moonlight bars
Is blurred with the fluff its long death strewed
In the crumpled fern; and far off something falls.
If the firs forget their breath, if the leaf that perishes
Holds, a bud, to spring; sleeps, fallen, under snow—
It is never still. The darkness quakes with blood;
From its pulse the dark eyes of the hunter glow
Green as their forest, fading images
Of the dream in the firelight: shudder of the coals
In their short Hell, vined skeleton
Of the charcoal-burner dozing in the snow.
Hänsel, to map the hard way, cast his bones
Up clouds to Paradise; His sparrows ate
And he plunged home, past peat and measures, to his kin
Furred in the sooty darkness of the cave
Where the old gods nodded. How the devil's beard
Coiled round the dreaming Hänsel, till his limbs
Grew gnarled as a fakir's on the spindling Cross

The missions rowed from Asia: eternal corpse
Of the Scapegoat, gay with His blood's watered beads,
Red wax in the new snow (strange to His warmed stare);
The wooden mother and the choir of saints, His stars;
And God and His barons, always, iron behind.
Gorged Hänsel felt His blood burn thin as air
In a belly swollen with the airy kine;
How many ages boiled Christ's bark for soup!
Giddy with emptiness, a second wife
Scolding the great-eyed children of a ghost,
He sends them, in his tale, not out to death
(Godfather Death, the reaping messenger),
Nor to the devil cringing in the gloom,
Shifting his barred hooves with a crunch like snow—
But to a king: the blind untroubled Might
Renting a destiny to men on terms—
Come, mend me and wed half of me, my son!
Behind, the headsman fondles his gnawn block.
So men have won a kingdom—there are kings;
Are giants, warlocks, the unburied dead
Invulnerable to any power—the Necessity
Men spring from, die under: the unbroken wood.

Noon, the gold sun of hens and aldermen
Inked black as India, on the green ground,
Our patterns, homely, mercenary, magnified—
Bewitching as the water of Friar Bacon's glass.
(*Our* farmer fooled the devil with a turnip,
Our tailor won a queen with seven flies;
Mouser and mousie and a tub of fat
Kept house together—and a louse, a louse
Brewed small beer in an eggshell with a flea.)
But at evening the poor light, far-off, fantastic—
Sun of misers and of mermen, the last foolish gold
Of soldiers wandering through the country with a crutch—
Scattered its leagues of shadows on the plots
Where life, horned sooty lantern patched with eyes,

Hides more than it illumines, dreams the hordes
Of imps and angels, all of its own hue.
In the great world everything is just the same
Or just the opposite, we found (we never went).
The tinkers, peddlers brought their pinch of salt:
In our mouths the mill of the unresting sea
Ground till their very sores were thirsty.
Quaking below like quicksand, there is fire—
The dowser's twig dips not to water but to Hell;
And the Father, uncomfortable overseer,
Shakes from the rain-clouds Heaven's branding bolt.
Beyond, the Alps ring, avalanche on avalanche,
And the lost palmers freeze to bliss, a smile
Baring their poor teeth, blackened as the skulls
Of sanctuaries—splinters of the Cross, the Ark, the Tree
Jut from a saint's set jawbone, to put out
With one bought vision many a purging fire.
As the circles spread, the stone hopes like a child.
The weak look to the helpless for their aid—
The beasts who, ruled by their god, Death,
Bury the son with their enchanted thanks
For the act outside their possibility:
The victim spared, the labors sweated through, for love
Neither for mate nor litter, but for—anything.
When had it mattered whom we helped? It always paid.
When the dead man's heart broke they found written there
(He could not write): *The wish has made it so.*
Or so he wished. The platter appliquéd
With meals for parents, scraps for children, gristle
For Towser, a poor dog; the walnut jetting wine;
The broom that, fretting for a master, swept a world;
The spear that, weeping for a master, killed a child;
And gold to bury, from the deepest mines—
These neither to wisdom nor to virtue, but to Grace,
The son remembered in the will of God—
These were wishes. The glass in which I saw
Somewhere else, someone else: the field upon which sprawled

Dead, and the ruler of the dead, my twin—
Were wishes? Hänsel, by the eternal sea,
Said to the flounder for his first wish, *Let me wish
And let my wish be granted;* it was granted.
Granted, granted. . . . Poor Hänsel, once too powerless
To shelter your own children from the cold
Or quiet their bellies with the thinnest gruel,
It was not power that you lacked, but wishes.
Had you not learned—have we not learned, from tales
Neither of beasts nor kingdoms nor their Lord,
But of our own hearts, the realm of death—
Neither to rule nor die? to change, to change!

[1946]

A Camp in the Prussian Forest

I walk beside the prisoners to the road.
Load on puffed load,
Their corpses, stacked like sodden wood,
Lie barred or galled with blood

By the charred warehouse. No one comes today
In the old way
To knock the fillings from their teeth;
The dark, coned, common wreath

Is plaited for their grave—a kind of grief.
The living leaf
Clings to the planted profitable
Pine if it is able;

The boughs sigh, mile on green, calm, breathing mile,
From this dead file
The planners ruled for them. . . . One year
They sent a million here:

Here men were drunk like water, burnt like wood.
The fat of good
And evil, the breast's star of hope
Were rendered into soap.

I paint the star I sawed from yellow pine—
And plant the sign
In soil that does not yet refuse
Its usual Jews

Their first asylum. But the white, dwarfed star—
This dead white star—
Hides nothing, pays for nothing; smoke
Fouls it, a yellow joke,

The needles of the wreath are chalked with ash,
A filmy trash
Litters the black woods with the death
Of men; and one last breath

Curls from the monstrous chimney. . . . I laugh aloud
Again and again;
The star laughs from its rotting shroud
Of flesh. O star of men!

[1946]

Eighth Air Force

If, in an odd angle of the hutment,
A puppy laps the water from a can
Of flowers, and the drunk sergeant shaving
Whistles *O Paradiso!*—shall I say that man
Is not as men have said: a wolf to man?

The other murderers troop in yawning;
Three of them play Pitch, one sleeps, and one
Lies counting missions, lies there sweating
Till even his heart beats: One; One; One.
O murderers! . . . Still, this is how it's done:

This is a war. . . . But since these play, before they die,
Like puppies with their puppy; since, a man,
I did as these have done, but did not die—
I will content the people as I can
And give up these to them: Behold the man!

I have suffered, in a dream, because of him,
Many things; for this last saviour, man,
I have lied as I lie now. But what is lying?
Men wash their hands, in blood, as best they can:
I find no fault in this just man.

[1947]

A Ward in the States

The ward is barred with moonlight,
  The owl hoots from the snowy park.
The wind of the rimed, bare branches
  Slips coldly into the dark

Warmed ward where the muttering soldiers
  Toss, dreaming that they still sigh
For home, for home; that the islands
  Are stretched interminably

Past their lives—past their one wish, murmured
  In the endless, breathless calm
By the grumbling surf, by the branches
  That creak from the splintered palm.

In bed at home, in the moonlight,
  Ah, one lies warm
With fever, the old sweat darkens
  Under the upflung arm

The tangled head; and the parted
  Lips chatter their old sigh,
A breath of mist in the moonlight
  That beams from the wintry sky.

[1947]

Jews at Haifa

The freighter, gay with rust,
Coasts to a bare wharf of the harbor.
From the funnel's shade (the arbor
Of gourds from which the prophet, without trust,
Watched his old enemies,
The beings of this earth) I scrutinize

The hundreds at the rail
Lapped in the blue blaze of this sea
Who stare till their looks fail
At the earth that they are promised; silently
See the sand-bagged machine-guns,
The red-kneed soldiers blinking in the sun.

A machine-gun away
Are men with our faces: we are torn
With the live blaze of day—
Till we feel shifting, wrenched apart, the worn
Named stones of our last knowledge:
That all men wish our death. Here on the edge

Of the graves of Europe
We believe: truly, we are not dead;
It seems to us that hope
Is possible—that even mercy is permitted
To men on this earth,
To Jews on this earth. . . . But at Cyprus, the red earth,

The huts, the trembling wire
That wreathes us, are to us familiar

As death. All night, the fires
Float their sparks up to the yellow stars;
From the steel, stilted tower
The light sweeps over us. We whisper: "Ours."

Ours; and the stones slide home.
There is no hope; "in all this world
There is no other wisdom
Than ours: we have understood the world,"
We think; but hope, in dread
Search for one doubt, and whisper: "Truly, we are not dead."

[1947]

A Field Hospital

He stirs, beginning to awake.
A kind of ache
Of knowing troubles his blind warmth; he moans,
And the high hammering drone
Of the first crossing fighters shakes
His sleep to pieces, rakes
The darkness with its skidding bursts, is done.
All that he has known

Floods in upon him; but he dreads
The crooked thread
Of fire upon the darkness: "The great drake
Flutters to the icy lake—
The shotguns stammer in my head.
I lie in my own bed,"
He whispers, "dreaming"; and he thinks to wake.
The old mistake.

A cot creaks; and he hears the groan
He thinks his own—
And groans, and turns his stitched, blind, bandaged head
Up to the tent-flap, red
With dawn. A voice says, "Yes, this one";
His arm stings; then, alone,
He neither knows, remembers—but instead
Sleeps, comforted.

[1947]

The Breath of Night

The moon rises. The red cubs rolling
In the ferns by the rotten oak
Stare over a marsh and a meadow
To the farm's white wisp of smoke.

A spark burns, high in heaven.
Deer thread the blossoming rows
Of the old orchard, rabbits
Hop by the well-curb. The cock crows

From the tree by the widow's walk;
Two stars, in the trees to the west,
Are snared, and an owl's soft cry
Runs like a breath through the forest.

Here too, though death is hushed, though joy
Obscures, like night, their wars,
The beings of this world are swept
By the Strife that moves the stars.

[1947]

Lady Bates

The lightning of a summer
Storm wakes, in her clay cave
At the end of the weeds, past the mock-orange tree—
Where she would come barefooted, curled-up-footed
Over the green, grained, rotting fruit
To eat blackberries, a scratched handful—
The little Lady Bates.
You have played too long today.
Open your eyes, Lady.
                     Is it a dream
Like the ones your mother used to talk away
When you were little and thought dreams were real?
Here dreams are real.
There are no more dreams, no more real—
There is no more night, there is no more day.

When the Lord God and the Holy Ghost and the Child Jesus
Heard about you, Lady,
They smiled all over their faces
And sang like a quartet: "Lady Bates,
Is it you, the little Lady Bates
Our minister, one Sunday evening,
Held down in the river till she choked
In a white dress like an angel's, red
With the clay of that red river? Lady,
Where are the two we sent to fetch your soul:
One coal-black, one high-yellow angel?
Where is night, where is day?
Where are you, Lady Bates?"

They looked for you east, they looked for you west,
And they lost you here in the cuckoo's nest
Eating the sweet white heart of the grass. . . .
You died before you had even had your hair straightened
Or waited on anybody's table but your own.
You stood there helping your step-mother
Boil clothes in the kettle in the yard,
And heard the girls go by, at play,
Calling to you in their soft mocking voices:
"Lady-Bug, Lady-Bug, fly away home."

You are home.
There is a bed of your own
Here where a few stones
Stick up in the tall grass dried to hay—
And one willow, at the end of summer,
Rustles, too dry to weep for you,
And the screech-owl sheers away
And calls, *Who, who*—you are afraid
And he is afraid: who else could see
A black ghost in the dark?
A black, barefooted, pigtailed, trifling ghost
With eyes like white clay marbles,
Who haunts no one—who lies still
In the darkness, waiting
While the lightning-bugs go on and off?
The darning-needles that sew bad girls' mouths shut
Have sewn up your eyes.
If you could open your eyes
You would see nothing.
                    Poor black trash,
The wind has blown you away forever
By mistake; and they sent the wind to the chain-gang
And it worked in the governor's kitchen, a trusty for life;
And it was all written in the Book of Life;
Day and Night met in the twilight by your tomb
And shot craps for you; and Day said, pointing to your soul,

"This *bad* young colored lady,"
And Night said, "Poor little nigger girl."

But Death, after the habit of command,
Said to you, slowly closing his hand:
"You're a big girl now, not even afraid
Of the dark when you awake—
When the day you sleep through
Is over, and you awake,
And the stars rise in the early evening
An inch or two over the grass of your grave—
Try to open your eyes;
Try to reach to one, to the nearest,
Reach, move your hand a little, try to move—
You can't move, can you?
You can't move. . . .
You're fast asleep, you're fast asleep."

[1948]

A Country Life

A bird that I don't know,
Hunched on his light-pole like a scarecrow,
Looks sideways out into the wheat
The wind waves under the waves of heat.
The field is yellow as egg-bread dough
Except where (just as though they'd let
It live for looks) a locust billows
In leaf-green and shade-violet,
A standing mercy.
The bird calls twice, *"Red* clay, *red* clay";
Or else he's saying, "Directly, directly."
If someone came by I could ask,
Around here all of them must know—
And why they live so and die so—
Or why, for once, the lagging heron
Flaps from the little creek's parched cresses
Across the harsh-grassed, gullied meadow
To the black, rowed evergreens below.

They know and they don't know.
To ask, a man must be a stranger—
And asking, much more answering, is dangerous;
Asked about it, who would not repent
Of all he ever did and never meant,
And think a life and its distresses,
Its random, clutched-for, homefelt blisses,
The circumstances of an accident?
The farthest farmer in a field,
A gaunt plant grown, for seed, by farmers,

Has felt a longing, lorn urbanity
Jailed in his breast; and, just as I,
Has grunted, in his old perplexity,
A standing plea.

From the tar of the blazing square
The eyes shift, in their taciturn
And unavowing, unavailing sorrow.
Yet the intonation of a name confesses
Some secrets that they never meant
To let out to a soul; and what words would not dim
The bowed and weathered heads above the denim
Or the once-too-often-washed wash dresses?

They are subdued to their own element.
One day
The red, clay face
Is lowered to the naked clay;
After some words, the body is forsaken. . . .
The shadows lengthen, and a dreaming hope
Breathes, from the vague mound, *Life;*
From the grove under the spire
Stars shine, and a wandering light
Is kindled for the mourner, man.
The angel kneeling with the wreath
Sees, in the moonlight, graves.

[1948]

Moving

Some of the sky is grey and some of it is white.
The leaves have lost their heads
And are dancing round the tree in circles, dead;
The cat is in it.
A smeared, banged, tow-headed
Girl in a flowered, flour-sack print
Sniffles and holds up her last bite
Of bread and butter and brown sugar to the wind.

Butter the cat's paws
And bread the wind. We are moving.
I shall never again sing
Good morning, Dear Teacher, to my own dear teacher.
Never again
Will Augusta be the capital of Maine.
The dew has rusted the catch of the strap of my satchel
And the sun has fallen from the place where it was chained
With a blue construction-paper chain. . . .
Someone else must draw the bow
And the blunderbuss, the great gobbler
Upside-down under the stone arrow
In the black, bell-brimmed hat—
And the cattycornered bat.
The witch on the blackboard
Says: "Put the Plough into the Wagon
Before it turns into a Bear and sleeps all winter
In your play-house under the catalpa."
Never again will Orion
Fall on my speller through the star

Taped on the broken window by my cot.
My knee is ridged like corn
And the scab peels off it.

We are going to live in a new pumpkin
Under a gold star.

There is not much else.
The wind blows somewhere else.
The brass bed bobs to the van.
The broody hen
Squawks upside-down—her eggs are boiled;
The cat is dragged from the limb.
The little girl
Looks over the shoulders of the moving-men
At her own street;
And, yard by lot, it changes.
Never again.
But she feels her tea-set with her elbow
And inches closer to her mother;
Then she shuts her eyes, and sits there, and squashed red
Circles and leaves like colored chalk
Come on in her dark head
And are darkened, and float farther
And farther and farther from the stretched-out hands
That float out from her in her broody trance:
She hears her own heart and her cat's heart beating.

She holds the cat so close to her he pants.

[1948]

When I Was Home Last Christmas . . .

When I was home last Christmas
I called on your family,
Your aunts and your mother, your sister;
They were kind as ever to me.

They told me how well I was looking
And clearly admired my wife;
I drank tea, made conversation,
And played with my bread, or knife.

Your aunts seemed greyer; your mother's
Lame unexpecting smile
Wandered from doily to doily;
Your dead face still

Cast me, with parted lips,
Its tight-rope-walker's look. . . .
But who is there now to notice
If I look or do not look

At a photograph at your mother's?
There is no one left to care
For all we said, and did, and thought—
The world we were.

[1948]

A Game at Salzburg

A little ragged girl, our ball-boy;
A partner—ex-Afrika-Korps—
In khaki shorts, P. W. illegible.
(He said: "To have been a prisoner of war
In Colorado iss a *privilege*.")
The evergreens, concessions, carrousels,
And D. P. camp of Franz Joseph Park;
A gray-green river, evergreen-dark hills.
Last, a long way off in the sky,
Snow-mountains.

Over this clouds come, a darkness falls,
Rain falls.
              On the veranda Romana,
A girl of three,
Sits licking sherbet from a wooden spoon;
I am already through.
She says to me, softly: *Hier bin i'*.
I answer: *Da bist du*.

I bicycle home in my raincoat
Through the ponchos and pigtails of the streets,
Bathe, dress, go down four flights of stairs
Past Maria Theresa's sleigh
To the path to the garden, walk along the lake
And kick up, dreamily, the yellow leaves
Of the lindens; the pigeons are cooing
In the morning-glories of the gardener's house,
A dragonfly comes in from the lake.

The nymphs look down with the faces of Negroes,
Pocked, moled with moss;
The stone horse has sunk in marsh to his shoulders.

But the sun comes out, and the sky
Is for an instant the first rain-washed blue
Of becoming: and my look falls
Through falling leaves, through the statues'
Broken, encircling arms
To the lives of the withered grass,
To the drops the sun drinks up like dew.

In anguish, in expectant acceptance
The world whispers: *Hier bin i'*.

[1949]

Transient Barracks

(1944)

Summer. Sunset. Someone is playing
The ocarina in the latrine:
You Are My Sunshine. A man shaving
Sees—past the day-room, past the night K.P.'s
Bent over a G.I. can of beets
In the yard of the mess—the red and green
Lights of a runway full of '24's.
The first night flight goes over with a roar
And disappears, a star, among mountains.

The day-room radio, switched on next door,
Says, "The thing about you is, you're *real*."
The man sees his own face, black against lather,
In the steamed, starred mirror: it is real.
And the others—the boy in underwear
Hunting for something in his barracks-bags
With a money-belt around his middle—
The voice from the doorway: "Where's the C.Q.?"
"Who wants to know?" "He's gone to the movies."
"Tell him Red wants him to sign his clearance"—
These are. Are what? Are.
                              "Jesus Christ, what a field!"
A gunner without a pass keeps saying
To a gunner without a pass. The man
Puts down his razor, leans to the window,
And looks out into the pattern of the field,
Of light and of darkness. His throat tightens,
His lips stretch into a blinded smile.

He thinks, *The times I've dreamed that I was back* . . .
The hairs on the back of his neck stand up straight.

He only yawns, and finishes shaving.
When the gunner asks him, "When you leaving?"
He says: "I just got in. This is my field."
And thinks: *I'm back for good. The States, the States!*
He puts out his hand to touch it—
And the thing about it is, it's *real*.

[1949]

A Sick Child

The postman comes when I am still in bed.
"Postman, what do you have for me today?"
I say to him. (But really I'm in bed.)
Then he says—what shall I have him say?

"This letter says that you are president
Of—this word here; it's a republic."
Tell them I can't answer right away.
"It's your duty." No, I'd rather just be sick.

Then he tells me there are letters saying everything
That I can think of that I want for them to say.
I say, "Well, thank you very much. Good-bye."
He is ashamed, and turns and walks away.

If I can think of it, it isn't what I want.
I want . . . I want a ship from some near star
To land in the yard, and beings to come out
And think to me: "So this is where you are!

Come." Except that they won't do,
I thought of them. . . . And yet somewhere there must be
Something that's different from everything.
All that I've never thought of—think of me!

[1949]

Seele im Raum

It sat between my husband and my children.
A place was set for it—a plate of greens.
It had been there: I had seen it
But not somehow—but this was like a dream—
Not seen it so that I knew I saw it.
It was as if I could not know I saw it
Because I had never once in all my life
Not seen it. It was an eland.
An eland! *That* is why the children
Would ask my husband, for a joke, at Christmas:
"Father, is it Donner?" He would say, "No, Blitzen."
It had been there always. Now we put silver
At its place at meals, fed it the same food
We ourselves ate, and said nothing. Many times
When it breathed heavily (when it had tried
A long useless time to speak) and reached to me
So that I touched it—of a different size
And order of being, like the live hard side
Of a horse's neck when you pat the horse—
And looked with its great melting tearless eyes
Fringed with a few coarse wire-like lashes
Into my eyes, and whispered to me
So that my eyes turned backward in their sockets
And they said nothing—
                              many times
I have known, when they said nothing,
That it did not exist. If they had heard
They *could* not have been silent. And yet they heard;
Heard many times what I have spoken

When it could no longer speak, but only breathe—
When I could no longer speak, but only breathe.

And, after some years, the others came
And took it from me—it was ill, they told me—
And cured it, they wrote me: my whole city
Sent me cards like lilac-branches, mourning
As I had mourned—
                    and I was standing
By a grave in flowers, by dyed rolls of turf,
And a canvas marquee the last brown of earth.

It is over.
It is over so long that I begin to think
That it did not exist, that I have never—
And my son says, one morning, from the paper:
"An eland. Look, an eland!"
                    —It was so.

Today, in a German dictionary, I saw *elend*
And the heart in my breast turned over, it was—

It was a word one translates *wretched*.

It is as if someone remembered saying:
"This is an antimacassar that I grew from seed,"
And this were true.
                    And, truly,
One could not wish for anything more strange—
For anything more. And yet it wasn't *interesting* . . .
—It was worse than impossible, it was a joke.

And yet when it was, I *was*—
Even to think that I once thought
That I could see it is to feel the sweat
Like needles at my hair-roots, I am blind

—It was not even a joke, not even a joke.

Yet how can I believe it? Or believe that I
Owned it, a husband, children? Is my voice the voice
Of that skin of being—of what owns, is owned
In honor or dishonor, that is borne and bears—
Or of that raw thing, the being inside it
That has neither a wife, a husband, nor a child
But goes at last as naked from this world
As it was born into it—

And the eland comes and grazes on its grave.

               This is senseless?
Shall I make sense or shall I tell the truth?
Choose either—I cannot do both.

I tell myself that. And yet it is not so,
And what I say afterwards will not be so:
To be at all is to be wrong.
             Being is being old
And saying, almost comfortably, across a table
From—
       from what I don't know—
                in a voice
Rich with a kind of longing satisfaction:
"To own an eland! That's what I call life!"

                    [1950]

The Orient Express

One looks from the train
Almost as one looked as a child. In the sunlight
What I see still seems to me plain,
I am safe; but at evening
As the lands darken, a questioning
Precariousness comes over everything.

Once after a day of rain
I lay longing to be cold; and after a while
I was cold again, and hunched shivering
Under the quilt's many colors, gray
With the dull ending of the winter day.
Outside me there were a few shapes
Of chairs and tables, things from a primer;
Outside the window
There were the chairs and tables of the world. . . .
I saw that the world
That had seemed to me the plain
Gray mask of all that was strange
Behind it—of all that *was*—was all.

But it is beyond belief.
One thinks, "Behind everything
An unforced joy, an unwilling
Sadness (a willing sadness, a forced joy)
Moves changelessly"; one looks from the train
And there is something, the same thing
Behind everything: all these little villages,
A passing woman, a field of grain,
The man who says good-bye to his wife—

A path through a wood full of lives, and the train
Passing, after all unchangeable
And not now ever to stop, like a heart—

It is like any other work of art.
It is and never can be changed.
Behind everything there is always
The unknown unwanted life.

[1950]

The Face

Die alte Frau, die alte Marschallin!

Not good any more, not beautiful—
Not even young.
This isn't mine.
Where is the old one, the old ones?
Those were mine.

It's so: I have pictures,
Not such old ones; people behaved
Differently then . . . When they meet me they say:
You haven't changed.
I want to say: You haven't looked.

This is what happens to everyone.
At first you get bigger, you know more,
Then something goes wrong.
You are, and you say: I am—
And you were . . . I've been too long.

I know, there's no saying no,
But just the same you say it. No.
I'll point to myself and say: I'm not like this.
I'm the same as always inside.
—And even that's not so.

I thought: If nothing happens . . .
And nothing happened.

Here I am.
                    But it's not *right*.
If just living can do this,
Living is more dangerous than anything:

It is terrible to be alive.

[1950]

Deutsch Durch Freud

I believe my favorite country's German.

I wander in a calm folk-colored daze; the infant
Looks down upon me from his mother's arms
And says—oh, God knows what he says!
It's baby-talk? he's sick? or is it German?
That *Nachtigallenchor:* does it sing German?
Yoh, yoh: here mice, rats, tables, chairs,
Grossmütter, Kinder, der Herrgott im Himmel,
All, all but I—
        all, all but I—
                speak German.

Have you too sometimes, by the fire, at evening,
Wished that you were—whatever you once were?
It is ignorance alone that is enchanting.
*Dearer to me than all the treasures of the earth
Is something living,* said old Rumpelstiltskin
And hopped home. Charcoal-burners heard him singing
And spoiled it all. . . . And all because—
If only he hadn't known his name!

In German I don't know my name.
                   I am the log
The fairies left one morning in my place.
—In German I believe in them, in everything:
The world is everything that is the case.
How clever people are! I look on open-mouthed
As Kant reels down the road *im Morgenrot*

Humming *Mir ist so bang, so bang, mein Schatz—*
All the nixies set their watches by him
Two hours too fast. . . .
                              I think, *My calendar's
Two centuries too fast,* and give a sigh
Of trust. I reach out for the world and ask
The price; it answers, *One touch of your finger.*

In all *my* Germany there's no *Gesellschaft*
But one between *eine Katze* and *ein Maus.*
What's business? what's a teaspoon? what's a sidewalk?
Schweig stille, meine Seele! Such things are not for thee.
It is by Trust, and Love, and reading Rilke
Without *ein Wörterbuch,* that man learns German.
The Word rains in upon his blessed head
As glistening as from the hand of God
And means—what does it mean? Ah well, it's German.
Glaube, mein Herz! A Feeling in the Dark
Brings worlds, brings words that hard-eyed Industry
And all the schools' dark Learning never knew.

And yet it's hard sometimes, I won't deny it.
Take for example my own favorite daemon,
Dear good great Goethe: *ach,* what German!
Very idiomatic, very noble; very like a sibyl.
My favorite style is Leupold von Lerchenau's.
I've memorized his *da und da und da und da*
And whisper it when Life is dark and Death is dark.
There was someone who knew how to speak
To us poor *Kinder* here *im Fremde.*
And Heine! At the ninety-sixth *mir träumte*
I sigh as a poet, but dimple as *ein Schuler.*
And yet—if it's easy is it German?
And yet, that *wunderschöne Lindenbaum
Im Mondenscheine!* What if it is in Schilda?
It's moonlight, isn't it? *Mund, Mond, Herz,* and *Schmerz*
Sing round my head, in *Zeit* and *Ewigkeit,*

And my heart lightens at each *Sorge,* each *Angst:*
I know them well. And *Schicksal! Ach,* you Norns,
As I read I hear your—what's the word for scissors?
And *Katzen* have *Tatzen*—why can't I call someone *Kind?*
What a speech for Poetry (especially Folk-)!

And yet when, in my dreams, *eine schwartzbraune Hexe*
(Who mows on the Neckar, reaps upon the Rhine)
Riffles my yellow ringlets through her fingers,
She only asks me questions: *What is soap?*
I don't know. *A suitcase?* I don't know. *A visit?*
I laugh with joy, and try to say like Lehmann:
"Quin-quin, es ist ein Besuch!"
                                        Ah, German!
Till the day I die I'll be in love with German
—If only I don't learn German. . . . I can hear my broken
Voice murmuring to *der Arzt: "Ich—sterber?"*
He answers sympathetically: *"Nein—sterbe."*

If God gave me the choice—but I stole this from Lessing—
Of German and learning German, I'd say: Keep your German!

The thought of *knowing* German terrifies me.
—But surely, this way, no one could learn German?
And yet. . . .
            It's difficult; is it impossible?
I'm hopeful that it is, but I can't say
For certain: I don't know enough German.

                                        [1950]

The Black Swan

When the swans turned my sister into a swan
  I would go to the lake, at night, from milking:
The sun would look out through the reeds like a swan,
  A swan's red beak; and the beak would open
And inside there was darkness, the stars and the moon.

Out on the lake a girl would laugh.
  "Sister, here is your porridge, sister,"
I would call; and the reeds would whisper,
  "Go to sleep, go to sleep, little swan."
My legs were all hard and webbed, and the silky

Hairs of my wings sank away like stars
  In the ripples that ran in and out of the reeds:
I heard through the lap and hiss of water
  Someone's "Sister . . . sister," far away on the shore,
And then as I opened my beak to answer

I heard my harsh laugh go out to the shore
  And saw—saw at last, swimming up from the green
Low mounds of the lake, the white stone swans:
  The white, named swans . . . "It is all a dream,"
I whispered, and reached from the down of the pallet

To the lap and hiss of the floor.
  And "Sleep, little sister," the swans all sang
From the moon and stars and frogs of the floor.
  But the swan my sister called, "Sleep at last, little sister,"
And stroked all night, with a black wing, my wings.

 [1951]

A Girl in a Library

An object among dreams, you sit here with your shoes off
And curl your legs up under you; your eyes
Close for a moment, your face moves toward sleep . . .
You are very human.
                            But my mind, gone out in tenderness,
Shrinks from its object with a thoughtful sigh.
This is a waist the spirit breaks its arm on.
The gods themselves, against you, struggle in vain.
This broad low strong-boned brow; these heavy eyes;
These calves, grown muscular with certainties;
This nose, three medium-sized pink strawberries
—But I exaggerate. In a little you will leave:
I'll hear, half squeal, half shriek, your laugh of greeting—
Then, *decrescendo,* bars of that strange speech
In which each sound sets out to seek each other,
Murders its own father, marries its own mother,
And ends as one grand transcendental vowel.

(Yet for all I know, the Egyptian Helen spoke so.)
As I look, the world contracts around you:
I see Brünnhilde had brown braids and glasses
She used for studying; Salome straight brown bangs,
A calf's brown eyes, and sturdy light-brown limbs
Dusted with cinnamon, an apple-dumpling's . . .
Many a beast has gnawn a leg off and got free,
Many a dolphin curved up from Necessity—
The trap has closed about you, and you sleep.
If someone questioned you, *What doest thou here?*
You'd knit your brows like an orangoutang

(But not so sadly; not so thoughtfully)
And answer with a pure heart, guilelessly:
I'm studying. . . .
                             If only you were not!
Assignments,
               recipes,
                            the *Official Rulebook*
Of Basketball—ah, let them go; you needn't mind.
The soul has no assignments, neither cooks
Nor referees: it wastes its time.
                                    It wastes its time.
Here in this enclave there are centuries
For you to waste: the short and narrow stream
Of Life meanders into a thousand valleys
Of all that was, or might have been, or is to be.
The books, just leafed through, whisper endlessly . . .
Yet it is hard. One sees in your blurred eyes
The "uneasy half-soul" Kipling saw in dogs'.
One sees it, in the glass, in one's own eyes.
In rooms alone, in galleries, in libraries,
In tears, in searchings of the heart, in staggering joys
We memorize once more our old creation,
Humanity: with what yawns the unwilling
Flesh puts on its spirit, O my sister!

So many dreams! And not one troubles
Your sleep of life? no self stares shadowily
From these worn hexahedrons, beckoning
With false smiles, tears? . . .
                                Meanwhile Tatyana
Larina (gray eyes nickel with the moonlight
That falls through the willows onto Lensky's tomb;
Now young and shy, now old and cold and sure)
Asks, smiling: "But what is she dreaming of, fat thing?"
I answer: She's not fat. She isn't dreaming.
She purrs or laps or runs, all in her sleep;

Believes, awake, that she is beautiful;
She never dreams.
           Those sunrise-colored clouds
Around man's head—that inconceivable enchantment
From which, at sunset, we come back to life
To find our graves dug, families dead, selves dying:
Of all this, Tanya, she is innocent.
For nineteen years she's faced reality:
They look alike already.
              They say, man wouldn't be
The best thing in this world—and isn't he?—
If he were not too good for it. But she
—She's good enough for it.
           And yet sometimes
Her sturdy form, in its pink strapless formal,
Is as if bathed in moonlight—modulated
Into a form of joy, a Lydian mode;
This Wooden Mean's a kind, furred animal
That speaks, in the Wild of things, delighting riddles
To the soul that listens, trusting . . .
             Poor senseless Life:
When, in the last light sleep of dawn, the messenger
Comes with his message, you will not awake.
He'll give his feathery whistle, shake you hard,
You'll look with wide eyes at the dewy yard
And dream, with calm slow factuality:
"Today's Commencement. My bachelor's degree
In Home Ec., my doctorate of philosophy
In Phys. Ed.
       [Tanya, they won't even *scan*]
Are waiting for me. . . ."
          Oh, Tatyana,
The Angel comes: better to squawk like a chicken
Than to say with truth, "But I'm a *good* girl,"
And Meet his Challenge with a last firm strange
Uncomprehending smile; and—then, then!—see
The blind date that has stood you up: your life.

(For all this, if it isn't, perhaps, life,
Has yet, at least, a language of its own
Different from the books'; worse than the books'.)
And yet, the ways we miss our lives are life.
Yet . . . yet . . .
                    to have one's life add up to *yet!*

You sigh a shuddering sigh. Tatyana murmurs,
"Don't cry, little peasant"; leaves us with a swift
"Good-bye, good-bye . . . Ah, don't think ill of me . . ."
Your eyes open: you sit here thoughtlessly.

I love you—and yet—and yet—I love you.

Don't cry, little peasant. Sit and dream.
One comes, a finger's width beneath your skin,
To the braided maidens singing as they spin;
There sound the shepherd's pipe, the watchman's rattle
Across the short dark distance of the years.
I am a thought of yours: and yet, you do not think . . .
The firelight of a long, blind, dreaming story
Lingers upon your lips; and I have seen
Firm, fixed forever in your closing eyes,
The Corn King beckoning to his Spring Queen.

[1951]

A War

There set out, slowly, for a Different World,
At four, on winter mornings, different legs . . .
You can't break eggs without making an omelette
—That's what they tell the eggs.

[1951]

In Those Days

In those days—they were long ago—
The snow was cold, the night was black.
I licked from my cracked lips
A snowflake, as I looked back

Through branches, the last uneasy snow.
Your shadow, there in the light, was still.
In a little the light went out.
I went on, stumbling—till at last the hill

Hid the house. And, yawning,
In bed in my room, alone,
I would look out: over the quilted
Rooftops, the clear stars shone.

How poor and miserable we were,
How seldom together!
And yet after so long one thinks:
In those days everything was better.

[1953]

Cinderella

Her imaginary playmate was a grown-up
In sea-coal satin. The flame-blue glances,
The wings gauzy as the membrane that the ashes
Draw over an old ember—as the mother
In a jug of cider—were a comfort to her.
They sat by the fire and told each other stories.

"What men want. . . ." said the godmother softly—
How she went on it is hard for a man to say.
Their eyes, on their Father, were monumental marble.
Then they smiled like two old women, bussed each other,
Said, "Gossip, gossip"; and, lapped in each other's looks,
Mirror for mirror, drank a cup of tea.

Of cambric tea. But there is a reality
Under the good silk of the good sisters'
Good ball gowns. *She* knew. . . . Hard-breasted, naked-eyed,
She pushed her silk feet into glass, and rose within
A gown of imaginary gauze. The shy prince drank
A toast to her in champagne from her slipper

And breathed, "Bewitching!" Breathed, "I am bewitched!"
—She said to her godmother, "Men!"
And, later, looking down to see her flesh
Look back up from under lace, the ashy gauze
And pulsing marble of a bridal veil,
She wished it all a widow's coal-black weeds.

A sullen wife and a reluctant mother,
She sat all day in silence by the fire.

Better, later, to stare past her sons' sons,
Her daughters' daughters, and tell stories to the fire.
But best, dead, damned, to rock forever
Beside Hell's fireside—to see within the flames

The Heaven to whose gold-gauzed door there comes
A little dark old woman, the God's Mother,
And cries, "Come in, come in! My son's out now,
Out now, will be back soon, may be back never,
Who knows, eh? *We* know what they are—men, men!
But come, come in till then! Come in till then!"

[1953]

The Meteorite

Star, that looked so long among the stones
And picked from them, half iron and half dirt,
One; and bent and put it to her lips
And breathed upon it till at last it burned
Uncertainly, among the stars its sisters—
Breathe on me still, star, sister.

[1954]

Windows

Quarried from snow, the dark walks lead to doors
That are dark and closed. The white- and high-roofed houses
Float in the moonlight of the shining sky
As if they slept, the bedclothes pulled around them.
But in some the lights still burn. The lights of others' houses.

Those who live there move seldom, and are silent.
Their movements are the movements of a woman darning,
A man nodding into the pages of the paper,
And are portions of a rite—have kept a meaning—
That I, that they know nothing of. What I have never heard
He will read me; what I have never seen
She will show me.
                    As dead actors, on a rainy afternoon,
Move in a darkened living-room, for children
Watching the world that was before they were,
The windowed ones within their windowy world
Move past me without doubt and for no reason.

These actors, surely, have known nothing of today,
That time of troubles and of me. Of troubles.
Morose and speechless, voluble with elation,
Changing, unsleeping, an unchanging speech,
These have not lived; look up, indifferent,
At me at my window, from the snowy walk
They move along in peace. . . . If only I were they!
Could act out, in longing, the impossibility
That haunts me like happiness!
Of so many windows, one is always open.

Some morning they will come downstairs and find me.
They will start to speak, and then smile speechlessly,
Shifting the plates, and set another place
At a table shining by a silent fire.
When I have eaten they will say, "You have not slept."

And from the sofa, mounded in my quilt,
My face on *their* pillow, that is always cool,
I will look up speechlessly into a—

It blurs, and there is drawn across my face
As my eyes close, a hand's slow fire-warmed flesh.

It moves so slowly that it does not move.

[1954]

Aging

I wake, but before I know it it is done,
The day, I sleep. And of days like these the years,
A life is made. I nod, consenting to my life.
. . . But who can live in these quick-passing hours?
I need to find again, to make a life,
A child's Sunday afternoon, the Pleasure Drive
Where everything went by but time; the Study Hour
Spent at a desk, with folded hands, in waiting.

In those I could make. Did I not make in them
Myself? The Grown One whose time shortens,
Breath quickens, heart beats faster, till at last
It catches, skips. . . . Yet those hours that seemed, were endless
Were still not long enough to have remade
My childish heart: the heart that must have, always,
To make anything of anything, not time,
Not time but—
                    but, alas! eternity.

[1954]

Children Selecting Books in a Library

With beasts and gods, above, the wall is bright.
The child's head, bent to the book-colored shelves,
Is slow and sidelong and food-gathering,
Moving in blind grace . . . Yet from the mural, Care,
The grey-eyed one, fishing the morning mist,
Seizes the baby hero by the hair

And whispers, in the tongue of gods and children,
Words of a doom as ecumenical as dawn
But blanched, like dawn, with dew. The children's cries
Are to men the cries of crickets, dense with warmth
—But dip a finger into Fafnir, taste it,
And all their words are plain as chance and pain.

Their tales are full of sorcerers and ogres
Because their lives are: the capricious infinite
That, like parents, no one has yet escaped
Except by luck or magic; and since strength
And wit are useless, be kind or stupid, wait
Some power's gratitude, the tide of things.

Read meanwhile . . . hunt among the shelves, as dogs do, grasses,
And find one cure for Everychild's diseases
Beginning: *Once upon a time there was*
A wolf that fed, a mouse that warned, a bear that rode
A boy. Us men, alas! wolves, mice, bears bore.
And yet wolves, mice, bears, children, gods and men

In slow perambulation up and down the shelves
Of the universe are seeking . . . who knows except themselves?

What some escape to, some escape: if we find Swann's
Way better than our own, and trudge on at the back
Of the north wind to—to—somewhere east
Of the sun, west of the moon, it is because we live

By trading another's sorrow for our own; another's
Impossibilities, still unbelieved in, for our own . . .
"I am myself still"? For a little while, forget:
The world's selves cure that short disease, myself,
And we see bending to us, dewy-eyed, the great
CHANGE, dear to all things not to themselves endeared.

[1941; *revised*, 1955]

Nestus Gurley

Sometimes waking, sometimes sleeping,
Late in the afternoon, or early
In the morning, I hear on the lawn,
On the walk, on the lawn, the soft quick step,
The sound half song, half breath: a note or two
That with a note or two would be a tune.
It is Nestus Gurley.

It is an old
Catch or snatch or tune
In the Dorian mode: the mode of the horses
That stand all night in the fields asleep
Or awake, the mode of the cold
Hunter, Orion, wheeling upside-down,
All space and stars, in cater-cornered Heaven.
When, somewhere under the east,
The great march begins, with birds and silence;
When, in the day's first triumph, dawn
Rides over the houses, Nestus Gurley
Delivers to me my lot.

As the sun sets, I hear my daughter say:
"He has four routes and makes a hundred dollars."
Sometimes he comes with dogs, sometimes with children,
Sometimes with dogs and children.
He collects, today.
I hear my daughter say:
"Today Nestus has got on his derby."
And he says, after a little: "It's two-eighty."

"How could it be two-eighty?"
"Because this month there're five Sundays: it's two-eighty."

He collects, delivers. Before the first, least star
Is lost in the paling east; at evening
While the soft, side-lit, gold-leafed day
Lingers to see the stars, the boy Nestus
Delivers to me the Morning Star, the Evening Star
—Ah no, only the Morning *News,* the Evening *Record*
Of what I have done and what I have not done
Set down and held against me in the Book
Of Death, on paper yellowing
Already, with one morning's sun, one evening's sun.

Sometimes I only dream him. He brings then
News of a different morning, a judgment not of men.
The bombers have turned back over the Pole,
Having met a star. . . . I look at that new year
And, waking, think of our Moravian Star
Not lit yet, and the pure beeswax candle
With its red flame-proofed paper pompom
Not lit yet, and the sweetened
Bun we brought home from the love-feast, still not eaten,
And the song the children sang: *O Morning Star—*

And at this hour, to the dew-hushed drums
Of the morning, Nestus Gurley
Marches to me over the lawn; and the cat Elfie,
Furred like a musk-ox, coon tailed, gold-leaf-eyed,
Looks at the paper boy without alarm
But yawns, and stretches, and walks placidly
Across the lawn to his ladder, climbs it, and begins to purr.
I let him in,
Go out and pick up from the grass the paper hat
Nestus has folded: this tricorne fit for a Napoleon
Of our days and institutions, weaving
Baskets, being bathed, receiving

Electric shocks, Rauwolfia. . . . I put it on
—Ah no, only unfold it.
There is dawn inside; and I say to no one
About—
       it is a note or two
That with a note or two would—
                say to no one
About nothing: "He delivers dawn."

When I lie coldly
—Lie, that is, neither with coldness nor with warmth—
In the darkness that is not lit by anything,
In the grave that is not lit by anything
Except our hope: the hope
That is not proofed against anything, but pure
And shining as the first, least star
That is lost in the east on the morning of Judgment—
May I say, recognizing the step
Or tune or breath. . . .
             recognizing the breath,
May I say, "It is Nestus Gurley."

                         [1956]

The Bronze David of Donatello

A sword in his right hand, a stone in his left hand,
He is naked. Shod and naked. Hatted and naked.
The ribbons of his leaf-wreathed, bronze-brimmed bonnet
Are tasseled; crisped into the folds of frills,
Trills, graces, they lie in separation
Among the curls that lie in separation
Upon the shoulders.
                    Lightly, as if accustomed,
Loosely, as if indifferent,
The boy holds in grace
The stone moulded, somehow, by the fingers,
The sword alien, somehow, to the hand.
                              The boy David
Said of it: "There is none like *that*."
                              The boy David's
Body shines in freshness, still unhandled,
And thrusts its belly out a little in exact
Shamelessness. Small, close, complacent,
A labyrinth the gaze retraces,
The rib-case, navel, nipples are the features
Of a face that holds us like the whore Medusa's—
Of a face that, like the genitals, is sexless.
What sex has victory?
The mouth's cut Cupid's-bow, the chin's unwinning dimple
Are tightened, a little oily, take, use, notice:
Centering itself upon itself, the sleek
Body with its too-large head, this green
Fruit now forever green, this offending
And efficient elegance draws subtly, supply,

Between the world and itself, a shining
Line of delimitation, demarcation.
The body mirrors itself.
                              Where the armpit becomes breast,
Becomes back, a great crow's-foot is slashed.
Yet who would gash
The sleek flesh so? the cast, filed, shining flesh?
The cuts are folds: these are the folds of flesh
That closes on itself as a knife closes.

The right foot is planted on a wing. Bent back in ease
Upon a supple knee—the toes curl a little, grasping
The crag upon which they are set in triumph—
The left leg glides toward, the left foot lies upon
A head. The head's other wing (the head is bearded
And winged and helmeted and bodiless)
Grows like a swan's wing up inside the leg;
Clothes, as the suit of a swan-maiden clothes,
The leg. The wing reaches, almost, to the rounded
Small childish buttocks. The dead wing warms the leg,
The dead wing, crushed beneath the foot, is swan's-down.
Pillowed upon the rock, Goliath's head
Lies under the foot of David.

Strong in defeat, in death rewarded,
The head dreams what has destroyed it
And is untouched by its destruction.
The stone sunk in the forehead, say the Scriptures;
There is no stone in the forehead. The head is helmed
Or else, unguarded, perfect still.
Borne high, borne long, borne in mastery,
The head is fallen.
                          The new light falls
As if in tenderness, upon the face—
Its masses shift for a moment, like an animal,
And settle, misshapen, into sleep: Goliath
Snores a little in satisfaction.

To so much strength, those overborne by it
Seemed girls, and death came to it like a girl,
Came to it, through the soft air, like a bird—
So that the boy is like a girl, is like a bird
Standing on something it has pecked to death.

The boy stands at ease, his hand upon his hip:
The truth of victory. A Victory
Angelic, almost, in indifference,
An angel sent with no message but this triumph
And alone, now, in his triumph,
He looks down at the head and does not see it.

Upon this head
As upon a spire, the boy David dances,
Dances, and is exalted.
                    Blessed are those brought low,
Blessed is defeat, sleep blessed, blessed death.

[1957]

The Woman at the Washington Zoo

The saris go by me from the embassies.

Cloth from the moon. Cloth from another planet.
They look back at the leopard like the leopard.

And I. . . .
        this print of mine, that has kept its color
Alive through so many cleanings; this dull null
Navy I wear to work, and wear from work, and so
To my bed, so to my grave, with no
Complaints, no comment: neither from my chief,
The Deputy Chief Assistant, nor his chief—
Only I complain. . . . this serviceable
Body that no sunlight dyes, no hand suffuses
But, dome-shadowed, withering among columns,
Wavy beneath fountains—small, far-off, shining
In the eyes of animals, these beings trapped
As I am trapped but not, themselves, the trap,
Aging, but without knowledge of their age,
Kept safe here, knowing not of death, for death—
Oh, bars of my own body, open, open!

The world goes by my cage and never sees me.
And there come not to me, as come to these,
The wild beasts, sparrows pecking the llamas' grain,
Pigeons settling on the bears' bread, buzzards
Tearing the meat the flies have clouded. . . .
                     Vulture,
When you come for the white rat that the foxes left,

Take off the red helmet of your head, the black
Wings that have shadowed me, and step to me as man:
The wild brother at whose feet the white wolves fawn,
To whose hand of power the great lioness
Stalks, purring. . . .
                    You know what I was,
You see what I am: change me, change me!

[1960]

Field and Forest

When you look down from the airplane you see lines,
Roads, ruts, braided into a net or web—
Where people go, what people do: the ways of life.

Heaven says to the farmer: "What's your field?"
And he answers: "Farming," with a field,
Or: "Dairy-farming," with a herd of cows.
They seem a boy's toy cows, seen from this high.

Seen from this high,
The fields have a terrible monotony.

But between the lighter patches there are dark ones.
A farmer is separated from a farmer
By what farmers have in common: forests,
Those dark things—what the fields were to begin with.
At night a fox comes out of the forest, eats his chickens.
At night the deer come out of the forest, eat his crops.

If he could he'd make farm out of all the forest,
But it isn't worth it: some of it's marsh, some rocks,
There are things there you couldn't get rid of
With a bulldozer, even—not with dynamite.
Besides, he likes it. He had a cave there, as a boy;
He hunts there now. It's a waste of land,
But it would be a waste of time, a waste of money,
To make it into anything but what it is.

At night, from the airplane, all you see is lights,
A few lights, the lights of houses, headlights,

And darkness. Somewhere below, beside a light,
The farmer, naked, takes out his false teeth:
He doesn't eat now. Takes off his spectacles:
He doesn't see now. Shuts his eyes.
If he were able to he'd shut his ears,
And as it is, he doesn't hear with them.
Plainly, he's taken out his tongue: he doesn't talk.
His arms and legs: at least, he doesn't move them.
They are knotted together, curled up, like a child's.
And after he has taken off the thoughts
It has taken him his life to learn,
He takes off, last of all, the world.

When you take off everything what's left? A wish,
A blind wish; and yet the wish isn't blind,
What the wish wants to see, it sees.

There in the middle of the forest is the cave
And there, curled up inside it, is the fox.

He stands looking at it.
Around him the fields are sleeping: the fields dream.
At night there are no more farmers, no more farms.
At night the fields dream, the fields *are* the forest.
The boy stands looking at the fox
As if, if he looked long enough—
                              he looks at it.
Or is it the fox that's looking at the boy?
The trees can't tell the two of them apart.

[1962]

THE LOST WORLD

I. Children's Arms

On my way home I pass a cameraman
On a platform on the bumper of a car
Inside which, rolling and plunging, a comedian
Is working; on one white lot I see a star
Stumble to her igloo through the howling gale
Of the wind machines. On Melrose a dinosaur
And pterodactyl, with their immense pale
Papier-mâché smiles, look over the fence
Of *The Lost World*.
                    Whispering to myself the tale
These shout—done with my schoolwork, I commence
My real life: my arsenal, my workshop
Opens, and in impotent omnipotence
I put on the helmet and the breastplate Pop
Cut out and soldered for me. Here is the shield
I sawed from beaver board and painted; here on top
The bow that only Odysseus can wield
And eleven vermilion-ringed, goose-feathered arrows.
(The twelfth was broken on the battlefield
When, searching among snap beans and potatoes,
I stepped on it.) Some dry weeds, a dead cane
Are my spears. The knife on the bureau's

My throwing-knife; the small unpainted biplane
Without wheels—that so often, helped by human hands,
Has taken off from, landed on, the counterpane—
Is my Spad.
        O dead list, that misunderstands
And laughs at and lies about the new live wild
Loves it lists! that sets upright, in the sands
Of age in which nothing grows, where all our friends are old,
A few dried leaves marked THIS IS THE GREENWOOD—
O arms that arm, for a child's wars, the child!

And yet they are good, if anything is good,
Against his enemies . . . Across the seas
At the bottom of the world, where Childhood
Sits on its desert island with Achilles
And Pitamakan, the White Blackfoot:
In the black auditorium, my heart at ease,
I watch the furred castaways (the seniors put
A play on every spring) tame their wild beasts,
Erect their tree house. Chatting over their fruit,
Their coconuts, they relish their stately feasts.
The family's servant, their magnanimous
Master now, rules them by right. Nature's priests,
They worship at Nature's altar; when with decorous
Affection the Admirable Crichton
Kisses a girl like a big Wendy, all of us
Squirm or sit up in our seats . . . Undone
When an English sail is sighted, the prisoners
Escape from their Eden to the world: the real one
Where servants are servants, masters masters,
And no one's magnanimous. The lights go on
And we go off, robbed of our fruit, our furs—
The island that the children ran is gone.

The island sang to me: *Believe! Believe!*
And didn't I know a lady with a lion?
Each evening, as the sun sank, didn't I grieve

To leave *my* tree house for reality?
There was nothing there for me to disbelieve.
At peace among my weapons, I sit in my tree
And feel: *Friday night, then Saturday, then Sunday!*

I'm dreaming of a wolf, as Mama wakes me,
And a tall girl who is—outside it's gray,
I can't remember, I jump up and dress.
We eat in the lighted kitchen. And what is play
For me, for them is habit. Happiness
Is a quiet presence, breathless and familiar:
My grandfather and I sit there in oneness
As the Sunset bus, lit by the lavender
And rose of sunrise, takes us to the dark
Echoing cavern where Pop, a worker,
Works for our living. As he rules a mark,
A short square pencil in his short square hand,
On a great sheet of copper, I make some remark
He doesn't hear. In that hard maze—in that land
That grown men live in—in the world of work,
He measures, shears, solders; and I stand
Empty-handed, watching him. I wander into the murk
The naked light bulbs pierce: the workmen, making something,
Say something to the boy in his white shirt. I jerk
As the sparks fly at me. The man hammering
As acid hisses, and the solder turns to silver,
Seems to me a dwarf hammering out the Ring
In the world under the world. The hours blur;
Bored and not bored, I bend things out of lead.
I wash my smudged hands, as my grandfather
Washes his black ones, with their gritty soap: ahead,
Past their time clock, their pay window, is the blue
And gold and white of noon. The sooty thread
Up which the laborers feel their way into
Their wives and houses, is money; the fact of life,
The secret the grown-ups share, is what to do

To make money. The husband Adam, Eve his wife
Have learned how not to have to do without
Till Santa Claus brings them their Boy Scout knife—
Nor do they find things in dreams, carry a paper route,
Sell Christmas seals . . .
                                   Starting *his* Saturday, his Sunday,
Pop tells me what I love to hear about,
His boyhood in Shelbyville. I play
What he plays, hunt what he hunts, remember
What he remembers: it seems to me I could stay
In that dark forest, lit by one fading ember
Of his campfire, forever . . . But we're home.
I run in love to each familiar member
Of this little state, clustered about the Dome
Of St. Nicholas—this city in which my rabbit
Depends on me, and I on everyone—this first Rome
Of childhood, so absolute in every habit
That when we hear the world our jailor say:
"Tell me, art thou a Roman?" the time we inhabit
Drops from our shoulders, and we answer: "Yea.
I stand at Caesar's judgment seat, I appeal
Unto Caesar."
                        I wash my hands, Pop gives his pay
Envelope to Mama; we sit down to our meal.
The phone rings: Mrs. Mercer wonders if I'd care
To go to the library. That would be ideal,
I say when Mama lets me. I comb my hair
And find the four books I have out: *The Food
Of the Gods* was best. Liking that world where
The children eat, and grow giant and good,
I swear as I've often sworn: "*I'll* never forget
What it's like, when *I've* grown up." A prelude
By Chopin, hammered note by note, like alphabet
Blocks, comes from next door. It's played with real feeling,
The feeling of being indoors practicing. "And yet
It's not as if—" a gray electric, stealing
To the curb on silent wheels, has come; and I

See on the back seat (sight more appealing
Than any human sight!) my own friend Lucky,
Half wolf, half police-dog. And he can play the piano—
Play that he does, that is—and jump so high
For a ball that he turns a somersault. "Hello,"
I say to the lady, and hug Lucky . . . In my
Talk with the world, in which it tells me what I know
And I tell it, "I know—" how strange that I
Know nothing, and yet it tells me what I know!—
I appreciate the animals, who stand by
Purring. Or else they sit and pant. It's so—
So *agreeable*. If only people purred and panted!
So, now, Lucky and I sit in our row,
Mrs. Mercer in hers. I take for granted
The tiller by which she steers, the yellow roses
In the bud vases, the whole enchanted
Drawing room of our progress. The glass encloses
As glass does, a womanish and childish
And doggish universe. We press our noses
To the glass and wish: the angel- and devilfish
Floating by on Vine, on Sunset, shut their eyes
And press their noses to their glass and wish.

II. A Night with Lions

When I was twelve we'd visit my aunt's friend
Who owned a lion, the Metro-Goldwyn-Mayer
Lion. I'd play with him, and he'd pretend
To play with me. I was the real player
But he'd trot back and forth inside his cage
Till he got bored. I put Tawny in the prayer
I didn't believe in, not at my age,
But said still; just as I did everything in fours
And gave to Something, on the average,
One cookie out of three. And by my quartz, my ores,
My wood with the bark on it, from the Petrified
Forest, I put his dewclaw . . .

                           Now the lion roars
His slow comfortable roars; I lie beside
My young, tall, brown aunt, out there in the past
Or future, and I sleepily confide
My dream-discovery: my breath comes fast
Whenever I see someone with your skin,
Hear someone with your voice. The lion's steadfast
Roar goes on in the darkness. I have been
Asleep a while when I remember: you
Are—you, and Tawny was the lion in—
In *Tarzan*. In *Tarzan!* Just as we used to,
I talk to you, you talk to me or pretend
To talk to me as grown-up people do,
Of *Jurgen* and Rupert Hughes, till in the end
I think as a child thinks: "You're my real friend."

III. A Street off Sunset

Sometimes as I drive by the factory
That manufactures, after so long, Vicks
VapoRub Ointment, there rises over me
A eucalyptus tree. I feel its stair-sticks
Impressed on my palms, my insteps, as I climb
To my tree house. The gray leaves make me mix
My coughing chest, anointed at bedtime,
With the smell of the sap trickling from the tan
Trunk, where the nails go in.
                              My lifetime
Got rid of, I sit in a dark blue sedan
Beside my great-grandmother, in Hollywood.
We pass a windmill, a pink sphinx, an Allbran
Billboard; thinking of Salâmmbo, Robin Hood,
The old prospector with his flapjack in the air,
I sit with my hands folded: I am good.

That night as I lie crossways in an armchair
Reading *Amazing Stories* (just as, long before,
I'd lie by my rich uncle's polar bear
On his domed library's reflecting floor
In the last year of the first World War, and see
A poor two-seater being attacked by four
Triplanes, on the cover of the *Literary
Digest,* and a Camel coming to its aid;
I'd feel the bear's fur warm and rough against me,
The colors of the afternoon would fade,
I'd reach into the bear's mouth and hold tight
To its front tooth and think, "I'm not afraid")

There off Sunset, in the lamplit starlight,
A scientist is getting ready to destroy
The world. "It's time for you to say good night,"
Mama tells me; I go on in breathless joy.
"Remember, tomorrow is a school day,"
Mama tells me; I go on in breathless joy.

At last I go to Mama in her gray
Silk, to Pop, to Dandeen in her black
Silk. I put my arms around them, they
Put their arms around me. Then I go back
To my bedroom; I read as I undress.
The scientist is ready to attack.
Mama calls, "Is your light out?" I call back, "Yes,"
And turn the light out. Forced out of life into
Bed, for a moment I lie comfortless
In the blank darkness; then as I always do,
I put on the earphones of the crystal set—
Each bed has its earphones—and the uneasy tissue
Of their far-off star-sound, of the blue-violet
Of space, surrounds the sweet voice from the Tabernacle
Of the Four-Square Gospel. A vague marionette,
Tall, auburn, holds her arms out, to unshackle
The bonds of sin, of sleep—as, next instant, the sun
Holds its arms out through the fig, the lemon tree,
In the back yard the clucking hens all cackle
As Mama brings their chicken feed. I see
My magazine. My magazine! Dressing for school,
I read how the good world wins its victory
Over that bad man. Books; book strap; jump the footstool
You made in Manual Training . . . Then we three
Sit down, and one says grace; and then, by rule,
By that habit that moves the stars, some coffee—
One spoonful—is poured out into my milk
And the milk, transubstantiated, is coffee.
And Mama's weekday wash-dress, Dandeen's soft black silk
Are ways that habit itself makes holy

Just as, on Sunday mornings, Wednesday nights, His will
Comes in their ways—of Church, of Prayer Meeting—to set free
The spirit from the flesh it questions.
                                                            So,
So unquestioned, my own habit moves me
To and through and from school, like a domino,
Till, home, I wake to find that I am playing
Dominoes with Dandeen. Her old face is slow
In pleasure, slow in doubt, as she sits weighing
Strategies: patient, equable, and humble,
She hears what this last child of hers is saying
In pride or bewilderment; and she will grumble
Like a child or animal when, indifferent
To the reasons of my better self, I mumble:
"I'd better stop now—the rabbit . . ."
                                                  I relent
And play her one more game. It *is* miraculous
To have a great-grandmother: I feel different
From others as, between moves, we discuss
The War Between the States. The cheerful troops
Ride up to our farmhouse, steal from us
The spoons, the horses—when their captain stoops
To Dandeen and puts Dandeen on his horse,
She cries . . . As I run by the chicken coops
With lettuce for my rabbit, real remorse
Hurts me, here, now: the little girl is crying
Because I didn't write. Because—
                                            of course,
I *was* a child, I missed them so. But justifying
Hurts too: if only I could play you one more game,
See you all one more time! I think of you dying
Forgiving me—or not, it is all the same
To the forgiven . . . My rabbit's glad to see me;
He scrambles to me, gives me little tame
Bites before he eats the lettuce. His furry
Long warm soft floppy ears, his crinkling nose
Are reassuring to a child. They guarantee,

As so much here does, that the child knows
Who takes care of him, whom he takes care of.

Mama comes out and takes in the clothes
From the clothesline. She looks with righteous love
At all of us, her spare face half a girl's.
She enters a chicken coop, and the hens shove
And flap and squawk, in fear; the whole flock whirls
Into the farthest corner. She chooses one,
Comes out, and wrings its neck. The body hurls
Itself out—lunging, reeling, it begins to run
Away from Something, to fly away from Something
In great flopping circles. Mama stands like a nun
In the center of each awful, anguished ring.
The thudding and scrambling go on, go on—then they fade,
I open my eyes, it's over . . . Could such a thing
Happen to anything? It could to a rabbit, I'm afraid;
It could to—
                    "Mama, you won't kill Reddy ever,
You won't ever, will you?" The farm woman tries to persuade
The little boy, her grandson, that she'd never
Kill the boy's rabbit, never even think of it.
He would like to believe her . . . And whenever
I see her, there in that dark infinite,
Standing like Judith, with the hen's head in her hand,
I explain it away, in vain—a hypocrite,
Like all who love.
                    Into the blue wonderland
Of Hollywood, the sun sinks, past the eucalyptus,
The sphinx, the windmill, and I watch and read and
Hold my story tight. And when the bus
Stops at the corner and Pop—Pop!—steps down
And I run out to meet him, a blurred nimbus,
Half-red, half-gold, enchants his sober brown
Face, his stooped shoulders, into the All-Father's.
He tells me about the work he's done downtown,
We sit there on the steps. My universe

Mended almost, I tell him about the scientist. I say,
"He couldn't really, could he, Pop?" My comforter's
Eyes light up, and he laughs. "No, that's just play,
Just make-believe," he says. The sky is gray,
We sit there, at the end of our good day.

[1963]

Thinking of the Lost World

This spoonful of chocolate tapioca
Tastes like—like peanut butter, like the vanilla
Extract Mama told me not to drink.
Swallowing the spoonful, I have already traveled
Through time to my childhood. It puzzles me
That age is like it.
             Come back to that calm country
Through which the stream of my life first meandered,
My wife, our cat, and I sit here and see
Squirrels quarreling in the feeder, a mockingbird
Copying our chipmunk, as our end copies
Its beginning.
           Back in Los Angeles, we missed
Los Angeles. The sunshine of the Land
Of Sunshine is a gray mist now, the atmosphere
Of some factory planet: when you stand and look
You see a block or two, and your eyes water.
The orange groves are all cut down . . . My bow
Is lost, all my arrows are lost or broken,
My knife is sunk in the eucalyptus tree
Too far for even Pop to get it out,
And the tree's sawed down. It and the stair-sticks
And the planks of the tree house are all firewood
Burned long ago; its gray smoke smells of Vicks.

Twenty Years After, thirty-five years after,
Is as good as ever—better than ever,
Now that D'Artagnan is no longer old—
Except that it is unbelievable.

I say to my old self: "I believe. Help thou
Mine unbelief."
                    I believe the dinosaur
Or pterodactyl's married the pink sphinx
And lives with those Indians in the undiscovered
Country between California and Arizona
That the mad girl told me she was princess of—
Looking at me with the eyes of a lion,
Big, golden, without human understanding,
As she threw paper-wads from the back seat
Of the car in which I drove her with her mother
From the jail in Waycross to the hospital
In Daytona. If I took my eyes from the road
And looked back into her eyes, the car would—I'd be—

Or if only I could find a crystal set
Sometimes, surely, I could still hear their chief
Reading to them from Dumas or *Amazing Stories;*
If I could find in some Museum of Cars
Mama's dark blue Buick, Lucky's electric,
Couldn't I be driven there? Hold out to them,
The paraffin half picked out, Tawny's dewclaw—
And have walk to me from among their wigwams
My tall brown aunt, to whisper to me: "Dead?
They told you I was dead?"
                                As if you could die!
If I never saw you, never again
Wrote to you, even, after a few years,
How often you've visited me, having put on,
As a mermaid puts on her sealskin, another face
And voice, that don't fool me for a minute—
That are yours for good . . . All of them are gone
Except for me; and for me nothing is gone—
The chicken's body is still going round
And round in widening circles, a satellite
From which, as the sun sets, the scientist bends
A look of evil on the unsuspecting earth.

Mama and Pop and Dandeen are still there
In the Gay Twenties.
                          The Gay Twenties! You say
The Gay Nineties . . . But it's all right: they *were* gay,
O so gay! A certain number of years after,
Any time is Gay, to the new ones who ask:
"Was that the first World War or the second?"
Moving between the first world and the second,
I hear a boy call, now that my beard's gray:
"Santa Claus! Hi, Santa Claus!" It *is* miraculous
To have the children call you Santa Claus.
I wave back. When my hand drops to the wheel,
It is brown and spotted, and its nails are ridged
Like Mama's. Where's my own hand? My smooth
White bitten-fingernailed one? I seem to see
A shape in tennis shoes and khaki riding-pants
Standing there empty-handed; I reach out to it
Empty-handed, my hand comes back empty,
And yet my emptiness is traded for its emptiness,
I have found that Lost World in the Lost and Found
Columns whose gray illegible advertisements
My soul has memorized world after world:
LOST—NOTHING. STRAYED FROM NOWHERE.
   NO REWARD.
I hold in my own hands, in happiness,
Nothing: the nothing for which there's no reward.

[1963]

The Mockingbird

Look one way and the sun is going down,
Look the other and the moon is rising.
The sparrow's shadow's longer than the lawn.
The bats squeak: "Night is here"; the birds cheep: "Day is gone."
On the willow's highest branch, monopolizing
Day and night, cheeping, squeaking, soaring,
The mockingbird is imitating life.

All day the mockingbird has owned the yard.
As light first woke the world, the sparrows trooped
Onto the seedy lawn: the mockingbird
Chased them off shrieking. Hour by hour, fighting hard
To make the world his own, he swooped
On thrushes, thrashers, jays, and chickadees—
At noon he drove away a big black cat.

Now, in the moonlight, he sits here and sings.
A thrush is singing, then a thrasher, then a jay—
Then, all at once, a cat begins meowing.
A mockingbird can sound like anything.
He imitates the world he drove away
So well that for a minute, in the moonlight,
Which one's the mockingbird? which one's the world?

[1963]

[89

Next Day

Moving from Cheer to Joy, from Joy to All,
I take a box
And add it to my wild rice, my Cornish game hens.
The slacked or shorted, basketed, identical
Food-gathering flocks
Are selves I overlook. Wisdom, said William James,

Is learning what to overlook. And I am wise
If that is wisdom.
Yet somehow, as I buy All from these shelves
And the boy takes it to my station wagon,
What I've become
Troubles me even if I shut my eyes.

When I was young and miserable and pretty
And poor, I'd wish
What all girls wish: to have a husband,
A house and children. Now that I'm old, my wish
Is womanish:
That the boy putting groceries in my car

See me. It bewilders me he doesn't see me.
For so many years
I was good enough to eat: the world looked at me
And its mouth watered. How often they have undressed me,
The eyes of strangers!
And, holding their flesh within my flesh, their vile

Imaginings within my imagining,
I too have taken

The chance of life. Now the boy pats my dog
And we start home. Now I am good.
The last mistaken,
Ecstatic, accidental bliss, the blind

Happiness that, bursting, leaves upon the palm
Some soap and water—
It was so long ago, back in some Gay
Twenties, Nineties, I don't know . . . Today I miss
My lovely daughter
Away at school, my sons away at school,

My husband away at work—I wish for them.
The dog, the maid,
And I go through the sure unvarying days
At home in them. As I look at my life,
I am afraid
Only that it will change, as I am changing:

I am afraid, this morning, of my face.
It looks at me
From the rear-view mirror, with the eyes I hate,
The smile I hate. Its plain, lined look
Of gray discovery
Repeats to me: "You're old." That's all, I'm old.

And yet I'm afraid, as I was at the funeral
I went to yesterday.
My friend's cold made-up face, granite among its flowers,
Her undressed, operated-on, dressed body
Were my face and body.
As I think of her I hear her telling me

How young I seem; I *am* exceptional;
I think of all I have.
But really no one is exceptional,
No one has anything, I'm anybody,
I stand beside my grave
Confused with my life, that is commonplace and solitary.

[1963]

In Galleries

The guard has a right to despair. He stands by God
Being tickled by the Madonna; the baby laughs
And pushes himself away from his mother.
The lines and hollows of the piece of stone
Are human to people: their hearts go out to it.
But the guard has no one to make him human—
They walk through him as if he were a reflection.
The guard does not see them either, you are sure,
But he notices when someone touches something
And tells him not to; otherwise he stands
Blind, silent, among the people who go by
Indistinguishably, like minutes, like the hours.
Slowly the days go by, the years go by
Quickly: how many minutes does it take
To make a guard's hair uniformly gray?

But in Italy, sometimes, a guard is different.
He is poorer than a guard would be at home—
How cheap his old uniform is, how dirty!
He is a fountain of Italian:
He pulls back a curtain, shows you where to stand,
Cajoles you back to the Ludovisi Throne
To show you the side people forget to look at—
And exclaiming hopefully, vivaciously,
Bellissima! he shows you that in the smashed
Head of the crouching Venus the untouched lips
Are still parted hopefully, vivaciously,
In a girl's clear smile. He speaks and smiles;
And whether or not you understand Italian,

You understand he is human, and still hopes—
And, smiling, repeating his *Bellissima!*
You give him a dime's worth of aluminum.

You may even see a guard who is dumb, whose rapt
Smile, curtain-pulling-back, place-indication,
Plain conviction that he guards a miracle
Are easier to understand than Italian.
His gestures are full of faith in—of faith.
When at last he takes a magnifying glass
From the shiny pocket of his uniform
And shows you that in the painting of a woman
Who holds in her arms the death of the world
The something on the man's arm is the woman's
Tear, you and the man and the woman and the guard
Are dumbly one. You say *Bellissima!*
Bellissima! and give him his own rapt,
Dumb, human smile, convinced he guards
A miracle. Leaving, you hand the man
A quarter's worth of nickel and aluminum.

[1964]

The Old and the New Masters

About suffering, about adoration, the old masters
Disagree. When someone suffers, no one else eats
Or walks or opens the window—no one breathes
As the sufferers watch the sufferer.
In *St. Sebastian Mourned by St. Irene*
The flame of one torch is the only light.
All the eyes except the maidservant's (she weeps
And covers them with a cloth) are fixed on the shaft
Set in his chest like a column; St. Irene's
Hands are spread in the gesture of the Madonna,
Revealing, accepting, what she does not understand.
Her hands say: "Lo! Behold!"
Beside her a monk's hooded head is bowed, his hands
Are put together in the work of mourning.
It is as if they were still looking at the lance
Piercing the side of Christ, nailed on his cross.
The same nails pierce all their hands and feet, the same
Thin blood, mixed with water, trickles from their sides.
The taste of vinegar is on every tongue
That gasps, "My God, my God, why hast Thou forsaken me?"
They watch, they are, the one thing in the world.

So, earlier, everything is pointed
In van der Goes' *Nativity,* toward the naked
Shining baby, like the needle of a compass.
The different orders and sizes of the world:
The angels like Little People, perched in the rafters
Or hovering in mid-air like hummingbirds;
The shepherds, so big and crude, so plainly adoring;

The medium-sized donor, his little family,
And their big patron saints; the Virgin who kneels
Before her child in worship; the Magi out in the hills
With their camels—they ask directions, and have pointed out
By a man kneeling, the true way; the ox
And the donkey, two heads in the manger
So much greater than a human head, who also adore;
Even the offerings, a sheaf of wheat,
A jar and a glass of flowers, are absolutely still
In natural concentration, as they take their part
In the salvation of the natural world.
The time of the world concentrates
On this one instant: far off in the rocks
You can see Mary and Joseph and their donkey
Coming to Bethlehem; on the grassy hillside
Where their flocks are grazing, the shepherds gesticulate
In wonder at the star; and so many hundreds
Of years in the future, the donor, his wife,
And their children are kneeling, looking: everything
That was or will be in the world is fixed
On its small, helpless, human center.

After a while the masters show the crucifixion
In one corner of the canvas: the men come to see
What is important, see that it is not important.
The new masters paint a subject as they please,
And Veronese is prosecuted by the Inquisition
For the dogs playing at the feet of Christ,
The earth is a planet among galaxies.
Later Christ disappears, the dogs disappear: in abstract
Understanding, without adoration, the last master puts
Colors on canvas, a picture of the universe
In which a bright spot somewhere in the corner
Is the small radioactive planet men called Earth.

[1965]

The Lost Children

Two little girls, one fair, one dark,
One alive, one dead, are running hand in hand
Through a sunny house. The two are dressed
In red and white gingham, with puffed sleeves and sashes.
They run away from me . . . But I am happy;
When I wake I feel no sadness, only delight.
I've seen them again, and I am comforted
That, somewhere, they still are.

It is strange
To carry inside you someone else's body;
To know it before it's born;
To see at last that it's a boy or girl, and perfect;
To bathe it and dress it; to watch it
Nurse at your breast, till you almost know it
Better than you know yourself—better than it knows itself.
You own it as you made it.
You are the authority upon it.

But as the child learns
To take care of herself, you know her less.
Her accidents, adventures are her own,
You lose track of them. Still, you know more
About her than anyone *except* her.

Little by little the child in her dies.
You say, "I have lost a child, but gained a friend."
You feel yourself gradually discarded.
She argues with you or ignores you

Or is kind to you. She who begged to follow you
Anywhere, just so long as it was you,
Finds follow the leader no more fun.
She makes few demands; you are grateful for the few.

The young person who writes once a week
Is the authority upon herself.
She sits in my living room and shows her husband
My albums of her as a child. He enjoys them
And makes fun of them. I look too
And I realize the girl in the matching blue
Mother-and-daughter dress, the fair one carrying
The tin lunch box with the half-pint thermos bottle
Or training her pet duck to go down the slide
Is lost just as the dark one, who is dead, is lost.
But the world in which the two wear their flared coats
And the hats that match, exists so uncannily
That, after I've seen its pictures for an hour,
I believe in it: the bandage coming loose
One has in the picture of the other's birthday,
The castles they are building, at the beach for asthma.
I look at them and all the old sure knowledge
Floods over me, when I put the album down
I keep saying inside: "I *did* know those children.
I braided those braids. I was driving the car
The day that she stepped in the can of grease
We were taking to the butcher for our ration points.
I *know* those children. I know all about them.
Where are they?"

I stare at her and try to see some sign
Of the child she was. I can't believe there isn't any.
I tell her foolishly, pointing at the picture,
That I keep wondering where she is.
She tells me, "Here I am."
                              Yes, and the other
Isn't dead, but has everlasting life . . .

The girl from next door, the borrowed child,
Said to me the other day, "You like children so much,
Don't you want to have some of your own?"
I couldn't believe that she could say it.
I thought: "Surely you can look at me and see them."

When I see them in my dreams I feel such joy.
If I could dream of them every night!

When I think of my dream of the little girls
It's as if we were playing hide-and-seek.
The dark one
Looks at me longingly, and disappears;
The fair one stays in sight, just out of reach
No matter where I reach. I am tired
As a mother who's played all day, some rainy day.
I don't want to play it any more, I don't want to,
But the child keeps on playing, so I play.

[1965]

Well Water

What a girl called "the dailiness of life"
(Adding an errand to your errand. Saying,
"Since you're up . . ." Making you a means to
A means to a means to) is well water
Pumped from an old well at the bottom of the world.
The pump you pump the water from is rusty
And hard to move and absurd, a squirrel-wheel
A sick squirrel turns slowly, through the sunny
Inexorable hours. And yet sometimes
The wheel turns of its own weight, the rusty
Pump pumps over your sweating face the clear
Water, cold, so cold! you cup your hands
And gulp from them the dailiness of life.

[1965]

Gleaning

When I was a girl in Los Angeles we'd go gleaning.
Coming home from Sunday picnics in the canyons,
Driving through orange groves, we would stop at fields
Of lima beans, already harvested, and glean.
We children would pick a few lima beans in play,
But the old ones, bending to them, gleaned seriously
Like a picture in my Bible story book.

So, now, I glean seriously,
Bending to pick the beans that are left.
I am resigned to gleaning. If my heart is heavy,
It is with the weight of all it's held.
How many times I've lain
At midnight with the young men in the field!
At noon the lord of the field has spread his skirt
Over me, his handmaid. "What else do you want?"
I ask myself, exasperated at myself.
But inside me something hopeful and insatiable—
A girl, a grown-up, giggling, gray-haired girl—
Gasps: "More, more!" I can't help hoping,
I can't help *expecting*
A last man, black, gleaning,
To come to me, at sunset, in the field.
In the last light we lie there alone:
My hands spill the last things they hold,
The days are crushed beneath my dying body
By the body crushing me. As I bend
To my soup spoon, here at the fireside, I can feel
And not feel the body crushing me, as I go gleaning.

[1969, *posthumous*]

A Man Meets a Woman in the Street

Under the separated leaves of shade
Of the gingko, that old tree
That has existed essentially unchanged
Longer than any other living tree,
I walk behind a woman. Her hair's coarse gold
Is spun from the sunlight that it rides upon.
Women were paid to knit from sweet champagne
Her second skin: it winds and unwinds, winds
Up her long legs, delectable haunches,
As she sways, in sunlight, up the gazing aisle.
The shade of the tree that is called maidenhair,
That is not positively known
To exist in a wild state, spots her fair or almost fair
Hair twisted in a French twist; tall or almost tall,
She walks through the air the rain has washed, a clear thing
Moving easily on its high heels, seeming to men
Miraculous . . . Since I can call her, as Swann couldn't,
A woman who is my type, I follow with the warmth
Of familiarity, of novelty, this new
Example of the type,
Reminded of how Lorenz's just-hatched goslings
Shook off the last remnants of the egg
And, looking at Lorenz, realized that Lorenz
Was their mother. Quacking, his little family
Followed him everywhere; and when they met a goose,
Their mother, they ran to him afraid.

Imprinted upon me
Is the shape I run to, the sweet strange

Breath-taking contours that breathe to me: "I am yours,
Be mine!"
   Following this new
Body, somehow familiar, this young shape, somehow old,
For a moment I'm younger, the century is younger.
The living Strauss, his moustache just getting gray,
Is shouting to the players: "Louder!
Louder! I can still hear Madame Schumann-Heink—"
Or else, white, bald, the old man's joyfully
Telling conductors they must play *Elektra*
Like *A Midsummer Night's Dream*—like fairy music;
Proust, dying, is swallowing his iced beer
And changing in proof the death of Bergotte
According to his own experience; Garbo,
A commissar in Paris, is listening attentively
To the voice telling how McGillicuddy met McGillivray,
And McGillivray said to McGillicuddy—no, McGillicuddy
Said to McGillivray—that is, McGillivray . . . Garbo
Says seriously: "I vish dey'd never met."

As I walk behind this woman I remember
That before I flew here—waked in the forest
At dawn, by the piece called *Birds Beginning Day*
That, each day, birds play to begin the day—
I wished as men wish: "May this day be different!"
The birds were wishing, as birds wish—over and over,
With a last firmness, intensity, reality—
"May this day be the same!"
      Ah, turn to me
And look into my eyes, say: "I am yours,
Be mine!"
   My wish will have come true. And yet
When your eyes meet my eyes, they'll bring into
The weightlessness of my pure wish the weight
Of a human being: someone to help or hurt,
Someone to be good to me, to be good to,
Someone to cry when I am angry

That she doesn't like *Elektra,* someone to start out on Proust with.
A wish, come true, is life. I have my life.
When you turn just slide your eyes across my eyes
And show in a look flickering across your face
As lightly as a leaf's shade, a bird's wing,
That there is no one in the world quite like me,
That if only . . . If only . . .
                  That will be enough.

But I've pretended long enough: I walk faster
And come close, touch with the tip of my finger
The nape of her neck, just where the gold
Hair stops, and the champagne-colored dress begins.
My finger touches her as the gingko's shadow
Touches her.
             Because, after all, it *is* my wife
In a new dress from Bergdorf's, walking toward the park.
She cries out, we kiss each other, and walk arm in arm
Through the sunlight that's much too good for New York,
The sunlight of our own house in the forest.
Still, though, the poor things need it . . . We've no need
To start out on Proust, to ask each other about Strauss.
We first helped each other, hurt each other, years ago.
After so many changes made and joys repeated,
Our first bewildered, transcending recognition
Is pure acceptance. We can't tell our life
From our wish. Really I began the day
Not with a man's wish: "May this day be different,"
But with the birds' wish: "May this day
Be the same day, the day of my life."

                       [1967, *posthumous*]

The Player Piano

I ate pancakes one night in a Pancake House
Run by a lady my age. She was gay.
When I told her that I came from Pasadena
She laughed and said, "I lived in Pasadena
When Fatty Arbuckle drove the El Molino bus."

I felt that I had met someone from home.
No, not Pasadena, Fatty Arbuckle.
Who's that? Oh, something that we had in common
Like—like—the false armistice. Piano rolls.
She told me her house was the first Pancake House

East of the Mississippi, and I showed her
A picture of my grandson. Going home—
Home to the hotel—I began to hum,
"Smile a while, I bid you sad adieu,
When the clouds roll back I'll come to you."

Let's brush our hair before we go to bed,
I say to the old friend who lives in my mirror.
I remember how I'd brush my mother's hair
Before she bobbed it. How long has it been
Since I hit my funnybone? had a scab on my knee?

Here are Mother and Father in a photograph,
Father's holding me. . . . They both look so *young*.
I'm so much older than they are. Look at them,
Two babies with their baby. I don't blame you,
You weren't old enough to know any better;

If I could I'd go back, sit down by you both,
And sign our true armistice: you weren't to blame.
I shut my eyes and there's our living room.
The piano's playing something by Chopin,
And Mother and Father and their little girl

Listen. Look, the keys go down by themselves!
I go over, hold my hands out, play I play—
If only, somehow, I had learned to live!
The three of us sit watching, as my waltz
Plays itself out a half-inch from my fingers.

[1965, *posthumous*]

INDEXES

Index of Titles

Index of First Lines